THE SCIENCE BEHIND
NATURAL
DISASTERS

HURRICANES

THE SCIENCE BEHIND KILLER STORMS

Dr. Alvin Silverstein, Virginia Silverstein,
and Laura Silverstein Nunn

Enslow Publishers, Inc.
40 Industrial Road
Box 398
Berkeley Heights, NJ 07922
USA

http://www.enslow.com

Library of Congress Cataloging-in-Publication Data

Silverstein, Alvin.
  Hurricanes: the science behind killer storms / Alvin Silverstein, Virginia Silverstein, and Laura Silverstein Nunn.
     p. cm.—(The science behind natural disasters)
  Includes bibliographical references and index.
  Summary: "Examines the science behind hurricanes, including how and where tropical storms form, the various types of tropical storms, how scientists track hurricanes, and provides hurricane safety tips"—Provided by publisher.
   ISBN-13: 978-0-7660-2971-2
   ISBN-10: 0-7660-2971-9
  1. Hurricanes—Juvenile literature. I. Silverstein, Virginia B. II. Nunn, Laura Silverstein. III. Title.
  QC944.2.S55 2009
  551.55'2—dc22
                        2008026264

Printed in the United States of America

10 9 8 7 6 5 4 3 2 1

To Our Readers: We have done our best to make sure all Internet Addresses in this book were active and appropriate when we went to press. However, the author and the publisher have no control over and assume no liability for the material available on those Internet sites or on other Web sites they may link to. Any comments or suggestions can be sent by e-mail to comments@enslow.com or to the address on the back cover.

♻ Enslow Publishers, Inc., is committed to printing our books on recycled paper. The paper in every book contains 10% to 30% post-consumer waste (PCW). The cover board on the outside of each book contains 100% PCW. Our goal is to do our part to help young people and the environment too!

Illustration Credits: AP/ Wide World Photos, pp. 1, 4, 8, 10, 16, 22 (top), 28, 32, 38, 41; Enslow Publishers, Inc., p. 7; John M. Evans, U.S. Geological Survey (USGS), Colorado District, p. 12; National Oceanic and Atmospheric Administration (NOAA), p. 22 (bottom); NOAA / National Hurricane Center, pp. 20, 36; NOAA's National Weather Service (NWS) Collection, p. 26; Orbital Imaging Corporation / Photo Researchers, Inc., p. 14; U.S. Air Force / Master Sgt. Michael A. Kaplan, p. 24.

Cover Illustration: AP/ Wide World Photos

CONTENTS

KATRINA
HITS
NEW ORLEANS

By 2005, New Orleans, Louisiana, had long been known for its Mardi Gras festivals and jazz music. It was a fun, happy city. But it was also a disaster waiting to happen.

New Orleans is near the Gulf of Mexico. Hurricanes often hit the Gulf area. People worried that someday the "big one" would do serious damage to the city. That is because New Orleans is *below* sea level. The waters of nearby wetlands, the Mississippi River, and Lake Pontchartrain rise during heavy rainstorms. In a hurricane they could overflow, flooding the streets of the city.

National Hurricane Center Director Max Mayfield points to Hurricane Katrina on a monitor showing the storm's center near Fort Lauderdale, Florida, just before 6 P.M. on August 25, 2005.

If New Orleans Is Below Sea Level, Why Isn't It Underwater?

New Orleans lies in a bowl-shaped area, from 2 to 6 meters (6 to 20 feet) below sea level. A system of levees (walls built from sand and dirt) protect the city. Floodwalls (structures made of steel and concrete) hold back the water. They are usually built on top of levees. In addition, pumping stations work to keep the land dry after a rainstorm.

Then, in August 2005, Hurricane Katrina smashed into New Orleans, causing unbelievable destruction. Days before, on August 23, the National Hurricane Center had warned southern Florida of a major tropical storm. Around noon on August 25, Palm Beach and a number of other counties began to evacuate. By that evening, Katrina was a hurricane.

Hurricane Katrina hit southern Florida hard. Winds blew up to 129 kilometers (80 miles) per hour, with as much as 12.5 to 38 centimeters (5 to 15 inches) of rain. Powerful winds and floodwaters knocked out electric power. The raging hurricane destroyed cars, buildings, and homes, and killed eleven people.[1]

During the night, Hurricane Katrina moved out over the Gulf of Mexico. But the warm Gulf waters only made the hurricane stronger. By August 27, Katrina was heading straight for the Gulf Coast. Louisiana, Alabama, and Mississippi were in a state of emergency. By the next day, the hurricane winds blew at over 274 kilometers (170 miles) per hour.[2]

New Orleans's mayor ordered residents to evacuate. Eighty percent of the New Orleans population evacuated before Hurricane Katrina hit.[3] But thousands were still in danger.

On August 29, Hurricane Katrina struck near the Louisiana-Mississippi border. By this time, the storm had weakened. But the winds were still blowing up to 201 kilometers (125 miles) per hour.[4] The whipping winds lifted the water of the ocean, lakes, and rivers and pushed it to the shore. These rising waters,

After hitting Florida, Katrina quickly strengthened over the warm waters of the Gulf of Mexico before it rammed into the Gulf Coast.

Crews from the Bay St. Louis Emergency Management Agency rescue the Taylor family from the top of their SUV in New Orleans as floodwaters rage around them.

called storm surges, flooded coastal areas. In a matter of hours, the floodwaters destroyed homes, roads, bridges, hospitals, and schools in Louisiana, Mississippi, and Alabama. The storm surges ranged from 3 to 8 meters (10 to 27 feet).[5]

In New Orleans, powerful storm surges rose over some of the levees and broke through others. As the levees crumbled, water rushed in from the Louisiana marshes and Lake Pontchartrain. The floodwaters covered 80 percent of the city, in some areas up to 6 meters (20 feet) deep. About two hundred fifty thousand people were left homeless.[6]

After New Orleans, Hurricane Katrina tore through Mississippi, leaving destruction in its path. As the storm moved inland, though, it continued to get weaker.

People will remember Katrina as one of the worst hurricanes in history. It caused more than $125 billion in damages.[7] Rebuilding has been a long, difficult process. Two years after Katrina hit, parts of New Orleans were still not fit for living. Many people had not rebuilt their homes and were living in trailers.

Is New Orleans Sinking?

Yes. Mud and sand, washed in by past floods, form the ground under the city. This kind of soft soil gradually settles. Since the city was built, efforts to keep floodwaters out have prevented more mud from adding to the sinking soil. So the city's ground level has been dropping by up to 2.5 centimeters (1 inch) or more each year.

Hurricane Katrina killed over eighteen hundred people in the Gulf Coast region.[8] Scientists have been studying Katrina and the emergency response to it. The information they have gathered is already helping people protect themselves from other hurricanes. When Hurricane Gustav struck New Orleans on September 1, 2008, people were expecting a storm like Katrina. However, Gustav was not as powerful, and the city was better prepared. The rebuilt levees held up. There was much less damage and far fewer deaths.

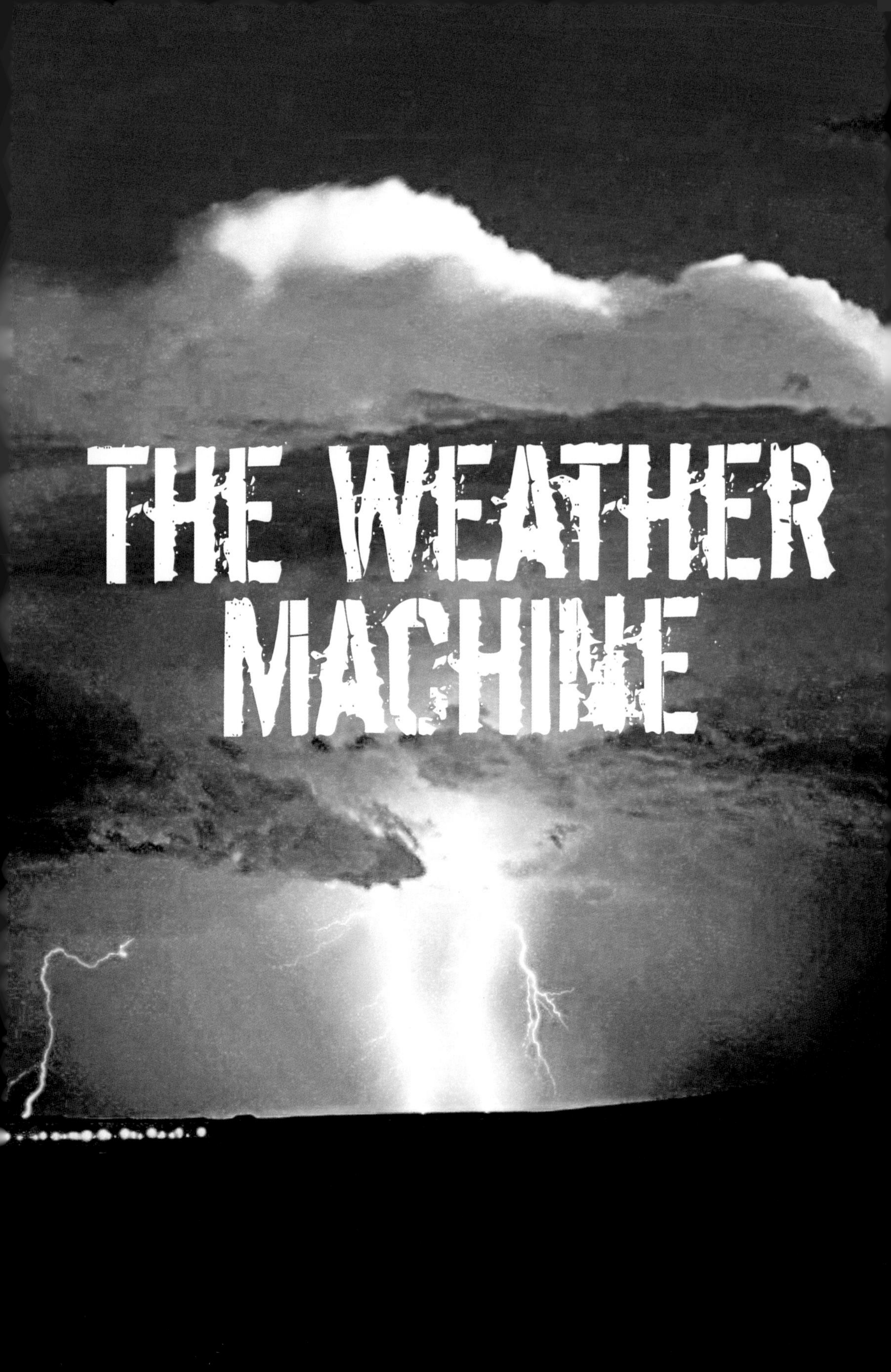
THE WEATHER
MACHINE

We live in an ocean of air.

We cannot see it, but it is moving around us all the time. Air is a mixture of gases that blankets the Earth and makes up part of the planet's atmosphere. Earth's atmosphere stretches out for hundreds of kilometers above the planet's surface. But the air we breathe is found in the lowest layer, just 10–18 kilometers (6–10 miles) thick.

Heat energy from the sun is the "engine" that drives our weather machine. This energy sends streams of air moving around our planet. Any changes in the atmosphere bring different kinds of weather. Extreme weather conditions, such as hurricanes, are the result of changes in the atmosphere.

All storms, whether they are hurricanes or thunderstorms, begin as air moving through the Earth's atmosphere. They are part of the planet's amazing weather machine.

Something in the Air

The atmosphere contains moisture, mostly in the form of an invisible gas called water vapor. The water vapor in the air comes mainly from the surface of oceans as part of a process called the water cycle. Sunlight heats up the oceans causing large amounts of water to evaporate, or change from a liquid to a gas. The warm, moist air rises into the atmosphere. As winds carry the moist air

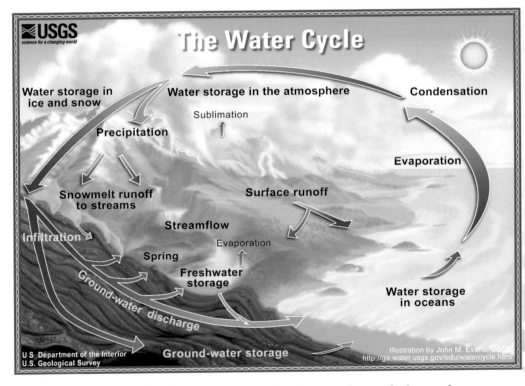

The water cycle is the movement of water on, in, and above the Earth. Earth's water is always changing states from liquid to vapor to ice and back again. The water cycle has been working for billions of years, and all life on Earth depends on it.

away, it begins to cool. Eventually the water may cool down enough that it condenses (turns into tiny water droplets) or freezes into ice crystals. These make up clouds, mist, and fog.

The water droplets or ice crystals in a cloud are constantly moving. When they bump into each other, they may join to form a larger droplet or crystal. When the water droplets or ice crystals become too heavy to stay up in the air, they fall. Thus, the clouds return water back to the Earth's surface as precipitation (rain, snow, hail, or sleet) to complete the water cycle.

Air in Motion

The air is made up of gas molecules, particles far too small to see without a very good microscope. The molecules in cold air move very slowly and are very close together. This makes them heavier than warm-air molecules, and they sink toward the ground. As gas molecules get heated, they move faster. The moving molecules bang into each other, forcing them to take up more room than when they were colder. When colder air sinks, it takes the place of warmer air and pushes the warmer air higher. Thus, warm air rises and cool air falls.

Warm air and cool air tend to gather in batches, called air masses. These air masses move around the planet. So the atmosphere swirls and bubbles like water heating in a pot on the stove.

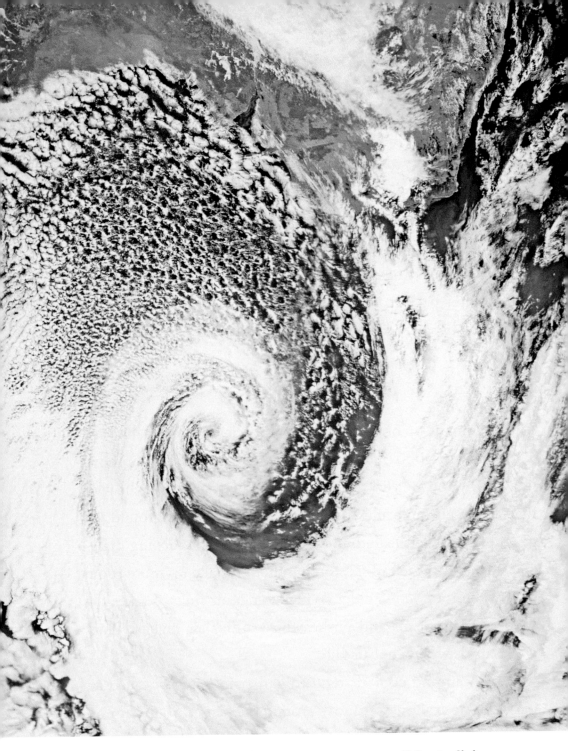

This satellite image shows a low-pressure system off Australia's
southern coast. Low pressure typically brings weather that is stormy
and humid. Such storm systems can increase in intensity to form a
cyclone (the name for a hurricane that is near Australia).

Under Pressure

You probably do not feel it, but air is constantly pressing down on you with great force. This force is called air pressure, or atmospheric pressure. Air pressure is the result of billions of molecules pressing down at a certain point on or above the Earth's surface.

Air pressure is highest at sea level because the air is densest, or thickest, there—it contains the most air molecules above it. If you climb a mountain, the air pressure decreases because the air becomes thinner (Air molecules spread out at higher levels so at any given point, there are fewer molecules above than if one were at sea level).

Weather forecasters often talk about "high-pressure systems" or "low-pressure systems." In high-pressure systems, air sinks down toward the Earth's surface. Air becomes drier as it falls, so the weather usually becomes stable and fair.

Low-pressure systems are more unstable. Warm air currents rise up into the sky in a swirling motion, forming clouds along the way. Hurricanes are low-pressure systems.

* It's a Fact! *

Some of the most violent storms start over tropical oceans. (The tropics are the areas near the equator between the Tropic of Cancer and the Tropic of Capricorn.) The sun's rays are the hottest there because that is the part of the Earth that is closest to the Sun. Oceans in the tropics hold on to heat better than land does. The warm water supplies energy that feeds the storms.

UNDERSTANDING HURRICANES

You will not hear about hurricane disasters in Kansas or the Sahara Desert. Hurricanes not only need heat to form, but they also need moisture—lots of it. The warm ocean waters of the tropics are perfect for the birth of a hurricane.

Meteorologists (weather scientists) use the term tropical cyclone to describe any storm over the tropical oceans that spins in a circle around a center of low pressure. Tropical cyclones are known by different names, depending on where they form. If these storms develop in the North Atlantic Ocean, the northeastern Pacific Ocean, the Gulf of Mexico, or the Caribbean Sea, they are called hurricanes.

High waves crash ashore in Shizuoka, Japan, on September 6, 2007, as Typhoon Fitow advanced toward Japan's main island of Honshu. These waves were part of Fitow's storm surge.

In the northwestern Pacific Ocean, near Japan and the Philippines, hurricanes are known as typhoons. Near Australia and in the Indian Ocean, they are called cyclones.

A Hurricane's Life Cycle

A hurricane goes through a series of four stages as it grows: tropical disturbance, tropical depression, tropical storm, and hurricane. Not all storms reach the higher stages.

Tropical disturbance: Tropical disturbances form over warm, tropical oceans, with water surface temperatures at least 26.5 degrees Celsius (80 degrees Fahrenheit). The warm surface water evaporates, sending water vapor into the air. As the moist air rises, it cools. Some of the water vapor condenses into water droplets, forming clouds. Clouds pile up high into the atmosphere, and thunderstorms develop.

Tropical depression: As the warm, moist air above the ocean rises, it creates an area of low air pressure. Cool heavier air from the surrounding area sinks, replacing the rising air. A cluster of thunderstorms joins to form a single large

What Does "Hurricane" Mean?

The term *hurricane* comes from "Huracan," the god of evil, named by an ancient Central American Indian group. Spanish colonists later changed the spelling to "hurricane."

weather system. Soon a whirlpool of hot, moist air is spiraling around a low-pressure center. As the swirling winds turn, they gather more energy from the warm water below. The wind speed rises. If the winds reach 61 kilometers (38 miles) per hour, the growing storm is ready to enter the next stage.

Tropical storm: The storm continues to grow stronger, and the winds blow faster. The strong winds draw up more heat and water vapor from the ocean surface, feeding the storm. Some of the water vapor condenses, producing heavy rain. Thunderstorms release heat, giving the storm even more power. Viewed from an airplane flying above the storm, the clouds have a distinct circular shape. If the wind speed reaches 119 kilometers per hour (74 miles per hour), the storm has reached the last stage—a hurricane.

Hurricane: The swirling winds of a hurricane surround the eyes an area of warm low-pressure air at the center. This is a calm area that may be from 10 to 65 kilometers (6 to 40 miles) across.

Why Do Hurricanes Swirl Around in a Circle?

Winds start blowing in a straight direction. But they curve because the Earth moves as it spins on its axis. This is known as Coriolis effect. The faster the winds blow, the more they curve. In a hurricane, winds blow so fast, they form spirals. In the Northern Hemisphere, the winds in a hurricane blow counterclockwise. In the Southern Hemisphere, they move clockwise.

Where Do Hurricanes Start?

The winds that blow over the tropical oceans are typically "easterlies"—winds that blow from east to west. Thunderstorms that develop in low-pressure areas disturb this wind flow, producing a wavelike movement. Meteorologists call it an easterly wave, or a tropical wave. About 80 percent of hurricanes in the Atlantic Ocean start in easterly waves over western Africa.[1]

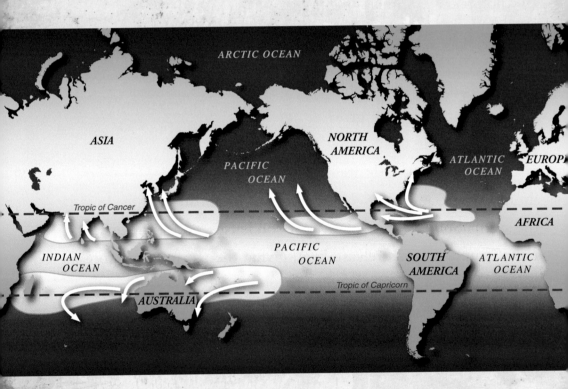

The shaded areas show where hurricanes form. The arrows represent the paths that they often take. The lighter the color of the ocean, the higher the sea-surface temperature.

In the eye of the storm it may be sunny with only light winds. To someone on the ground, it seems like the storm is over. But it is not.

The strongest winds blow around the edge of the eye, called the eyewall. Bands of thick clouds, called rainbands, swirl outward around the eyewall. As the storm moves, the area that was below the eye suddenly gets stormy again. The rainbands can produce more than 5 centimeters (2 inches) of rain per hour.

As it develops, a hurricane moves across the ocean. It usually travels northwest at a speed of 16 to 32 kilometers (10 to 20 miles) per hour. It may eventually reach a coast and move inland. As soon as the hurricane passes over land, however, its wind speed drops. Remember that the warm ocean waters supply a hurricane with energy. The air over land areas is cooler and drier, so the hurricane gets weaker. Soon it may become just a tropical storm, and eventually it dies out.

Sometimes a hurricane may change course and move back out over the ocean. Picking up energy, it may later hit the coast

Are Big Hurricanes More Powerful Than Small Ones?

Not always. Hurricane Andrew, which hit southern Florida in 1992, was the second-most destructive hurricane in U.S. history. But it was fairly small, measuring only 97 kilometers (60 miles) across, compared to the average hurricane, which covers an area 483 kilometers (300 miles) wide.[2]

This satellite image of Hurricane Katrina shows the storm's eye making landfall at 7:10 A.M., on August 29, 2005.

This towering mass of white clouds is part of Hurricane Katrina's eyewall, the area around the central eye. The strongest winds are found in the eyewall. The picture was taken on August 28, 2005, from a hurricane hunter airplane.

again in a different spot with greater force. This is what happened with Katrina, which first hit Florida, then moved over the Gulf of Mexico to hit the Gulf Coast even harder. A hurricane can last an average of three to fourteen days, and travel as many as 6,400 kilometers (4,000 miles).

Naming Hurricanes

Every year, meteorologists use a special alphabetical list of names for hurricanes. Different lists are used for hurricanes in the Atlantic and Pacific regions. The names are common first names in the languages of the regions where the storms strike.

Hurricane names are retired (no longer used) if a named storm causes a tremendous amount of damage or the loss of many lives. "Katrina," for example, will never be used again.

When Is Hurricane Season?

Hurricanes usually form at a certain time of the year, known as the hurricane season. Since hurricanes need warm, moist air to form, they usually develop during the summer and autumn months. The Atlantic hurricane season is from June 1 to November 30. The hurricane season for the northeast Pacific is May 15 to November 30.

WHEN A HURRICANE HITS

4

Every year, eighty to one hundred tropical storms develop around the world. About forty to sixty of them get strong enough to become hurricanes, typhoons, or cyclones.[1] And only a few of those ever reach places where people live.

More hurricanes hit some regions than others. In the northwest Pacific Ocean, for example, an average of twenty-eight tropical storms occur each year; nineteen of them become typhoons.[2] In the Atlantic Ocean, however, an average of only ten tropical storms develop every year, and six of them become hurricanes. Over a three-year period, the United States coast gets hit an average of five times by hurricanes, and two of them are major hurricanes.[3] When a hurricane hits land—no matter where—the effects can be disastrous.

A historic home was damaged September 24, 2005 by a tree downed by Hurricane Rita at Barksdale Air Force Base in Louisiana.

Whipping Winds

Hurricane winds are extremely powerful. Out at sea, the winds can blow up to 322 kilometers (200 miles) per hour. Although a hurricane loses energy when it moves over land, the winds still cause a lot of damage. Strong gusts of wind rip huge trees out of the ground. They toss cars and people through the air. The wind can even turn small objects, such as a road sign or a lawn chair, into deadly flying missiles.

Hurricanes are especially destructive when they hit an area where many people live. Hurricane Andrew, for example, had winds of 266 kilometers (165 miles) per hour when it reached the coast of southern Florida in 1992.[4] It passed through an area

This diagram shows how Hurricane Andrew's winds damaged this home's roof.

south of Miami that was filled with homes and businesses. Many of the buildings there were mobile

homes, which do not weigh as much as houses. They also are not well anchored to the ground. In some communities, more than 90 percent of mobile homes were completely destroyed.[6]

Storm Surges

Even though a hurricane's winds are dangerous, people are more likely to die from a storm surge. The winds of the storm push ocean waters toward the shore, forming a huge wave. The low air pressure also lifts the water, raising the level even higher. These forces combine with the normal ocean tides, forming a huge wall of water. Many hurricanes have produced storm surges more than 6 meters (20 feet) high.

The surging water smashes into buildings and washes out roads. The storm surge may also wash away beaches and remove the soil around the foundations of houses.

Heavy Rains

Hurricanes can cause serious flooding even without a storm surge. Their rainbands can dump 25 to 38 centimeters (10 to 15

When Hurricane Floyd came toward land in September 1999, its storm surge collapsed this pier at Daytona Beach, Florida.

inches) of rain in a twenty-four hour period. Bigger storms bring heavier rains—up to 51 centimeters (20 inches) or more. Such huge amounts of rainfall in a short amount of time can flood entire communities.

Heavy rains can also cause mudslides. Rain mixes with the soil on mountains and hillsides and forms mud. The mud flows downhill. Rocks break free, adding to the mixture. As the mudslide rushes down the mountain, it rips out trees and carries away houses. Down below, it buries everything in mud. Hurricane Mitch killed more than ten thousand people in 1998 due to mudslides caused by heavy rains.[7]

Tornadoes

Hurricanes can also bring tornadoes. These are small but very powerful storms. The winds of a tornado, or "twister," rapidly swirl around in a tall cloud that is funnel-shaped. Some hurricanes do not produce any tornadoes; others spawn, or form, many of them. Hurricane Katrina, for example, produced sixty-two tornadoes.[8] The tornadoes that come with hurricanes are not usually as powerful as those that form during thunderstorms in the Midwestern states.

What's the Damage?

Scientists use the Saffir-Simpson Hurricane Scale to

What Is the Difference Between Hurricanes and Tornadoes?

Hurricanes and tornadoes are both cyclones—powerful windstorms that spin in a circle. But they have major differences:

- Hurricanes form over the ocean. Most tornadoes form over land.

- Hurricanes are huge, often hundreds of kilometers wide. Tornadoes are usually much smaller, only 122 to 152 meters (400 to 500 feet) wide.

- Hurricanes last for up to two weeks. Tornadoes last for up to three hours.

- Hurricane winds are not as powerful as tornado winds. Tornado winds typically blow 320 to 480 kilometers (200 to 300 miles) per hour.

rank the strength of a hurricane. The scale rates a hurricane from Category 1 (least powerful) to Category 5 (most destructive). The rating is based on average wind speed. Each category also indicates the level of storm surge and how much damage scientists think the hurricane will do.

Hurricanes in categories 3, 4, and 5 are considered major hurricanes. They can cause widespread damage to property, severe inland flooding, and significant loss of life. Hurricanes can change categories as they gain or lose strength. That is what happened with Hurricane Katrina. Over the Gulf of Mexico, Katrina had become a Category 5, but it was down to Category 3 by the time it reached the Louisiana-Mississippi border as it moved inland.

Are Hurricanes Getting Worse?

Some studies have shown that the number of category 4 and 5 hurricanes has increased worldwide since the 1980s.[9] Many scientists believe this increase in severe storms is due to global-warming. They think our planet has been getting warmer. Since a warmer planet means warmer oceans, storms have become more powerful. Other scientists have a different idea as to why strong hurricanes have been recorded. They think that scientists have just gotten better at detecting and tracking hurricanes. Because technology has become so advanced, scientists can track hurricanes better and warn people in advance.

SAFFIR–SIMPSON HURRICANE SCALE

CATEGORY	WIND SPEED	STORM SURGE	DAMAGES
1	119–153 km/hr (74–95 mph)	1.2–1.5 m (4–5 ft)	• Some flooding • Little or no damage to building structures
2	155–177 km/hr (96–110 mph)	1.8–2.4 m (6–8 ft)	• Flooding of coastal roads • Some trees blown down • Damage to roof shingles, doors, and windows
3	179–209 km/hr (111–130 mph)	2.7–3.7 m (9–12 ft)	• Damage to house structures • Mobile homes destroyed • Severe flooding
4	211–249 km/hr (131–155 mph)	4–5.5 m (13–18 ft)	• Severe flooding inland • Some roofs ripped off • Major structural damage to lower floors of buildings
5	> 249 km/hr (>155 mph)	> 5.5 m (18 ft)	• Severe flooding farther inland • All trees and shrubs blown down • Mobile homes destroyed • Serious damage to building and house structures

TRACKING HURRICANES

Imagine a storm striking

where you live. It is a big one—a hurricane. You had no idea it was coming. Now you and your family have very little time to prepare yourselves.

Before the 1950s, there were no reliable methods for predicting the weather. People did not know when a hurricane was coming. Warnings could have saved many lives. In 1900, for example, an unexpected hurricane that hit Galveston, Texas, killed at least eight thousand people.[1]

Today, advanced technology allows weather forecasters to track a hurricane and warn people *before* it is about to hit.

Meteorologist Robbie Berg studies the movements of Hurricane Frances and Tropical Storm Gaston on different computer screens at the National Hurricane Center in Miami on August 31, 2004.

A Hurricane Warning Ignored

In 1502, Christopher Columbus was sailing to the Caribbean when he saw a hurricane coming. When he arrived at Santo Domingo, Columbus warned the governor. Columbus and his crew found safety on a nearby island. But the governor's fleet set sail right into the hurricane. About twenty of the Spanish ships were destroyed. Five hundred men lost their lives—including the governor.[2]

Weather Satellites

The National Hurricane Center has meteorologists watching twenty-four hours a day for developing hurricanes. Weather satellites orbiting the Earth often give the first clues that a hurricane is forming. These satellites carry instruments that take pictures of the planet and its atmosphere. By studying these images, meteorologists can spot hurricanes anywhere in the world. This allows the National Weather Service to issue warnings to people threatened by these storms. Hurricane warnings are sent out through radio, television, and the Internet.

Instruments can also measure temperatures on the ground, on the sea surface, and at different levels of the atmosphere. They can detect the direction and speed of the wind and the humidity in the air. Meteorologists use this technology to track a hurricane's path. However, hurricanes sometimes change direction unexpectedly.

Weather Radar

Weather radar collects information about cloud formation and precipitation. Radar sends out radio signals, which bounce off raindrops and ice crystals inside the clouds. The way these signals bounce shows the size and location of the clouds. The radio signals change depending on whether the clouds are moving toward or away from the radar. Meteorologists use this information to track where the weather systems are moving.

Hurricane Hunters

A lot of information about hurricanes also comes from "hurricane hunters." Airplane crews working for the National Oceanic and Atmospheric Administration (NOAA) and the Air Force fly right through raging hurricanes! The airplanes carry radar, computers, and weather instruments that record air temperature, air pressure, wind speed, and wind direction. The hurricane hunters can also get clues to the hurricane's path by dropping weather instruments from the plane. These devices

Is It a Hurricane Watch or a Hurricane Warning?

A hurricane "watch" is a National Weather Service alert that a hurricane is *possible* for a particular area within the next thirty-six hours. A hurricane "warning" is an alert that a hurricane is *expected* to reach land within twenty-four hours.

A hurricane hunter flies directly over the eye of a hurricane.

measure temperature, air pressure, and wind at different levels as they fall down through the hurricane toward the ocean.

Computer Models

Computer models are important tools that help predict where hurricanes will form and what they will do. Many different things can affect storms: air pressure, humidity, temperature, wind speed and direction, and ocean currents. These changing conditions all help determine how strong a hurricane will grow and whether or where it will hit the land. Today's powerful computers are very good at doing the complicated calculations.

The computers use weather information to calculate how a hurricane's conditions will change.

Meteorologists can use a number of different computer models to predict hurricanes. When Hurricane Katrina first hit South Florida, for example, forecasters predict that the storm would move over the Gulf of Mexico and gather strength. Fifty-six hours before landfall on the

Galveston Revisited

A monster hurricane hit Galveston, Texas on September 14, 2008. Hurricane Ike was 805 kilometers (500 miles) wide. At landfall its wind speed was 177 kilometers (110 miles) per hour—just under Category 3.[4] But unlike the 1900 hurricane, residents had several days of warning. Close to one million people evacuated successfully. The storm caused a lot of flooding and property damage, but relatively few deaths.

Gulf Coast, they knew it would strike southeastern Louisiana as a monster storm.[3] Their warnings made it possible to evacuate cities and save thousands of lives.

STAYING SAFE

An estimated 35 million people,

or 12 percent of the people in the United States, live in the southern coastal regions most threatened by Atlantic hurricanes.[1] As the coastal population continues to grow, the damages due to hurricanes also increase.

Scientists may not be able to prevent a hurricane from invading where people live. However, there are a number of things people can do to survive when a hurricane hits.

Emergency Plan

In case a hurricane hits, you and your family should have an emergency plan. There are probably special

Jason Ross, top, and John Heilig, bottom, board up a beach house on September 16, 2003, in Nags Head, North Carolina, as people prepare for a possible hit from Hurricane Isabel.

What Should You Do About Your Pets?

Try to take your pets and pet supplies with you if you have to evacuate pets. They likely will die if left on their own. Come up with a plan for them *before* there is an emergency.

Hurricane shelters usually will not take in pets. Look for hotels outside your local area that will accept pets. Make a list of animal boarders and veterinary offices that will keep animals in an emergency. Your pets should all have collars and identification tags.

hurricane shelters nearby. Find out where they are and the fastest way to get to them.

At home, keep a disaster supply kit handy. You will need items to keep you safe in case the power goes out or your neighborhood is flooded. Emergency supplies can get you through a few days stuck in your home or a shelter until regular services are working again. The kit should include:

- Flashlight and batteries
- Battery-operated radio
- First Aid kit
- Emergency food and water
- Special items for babies, the elderly, and pets
- Protective clothing, such as rain gear
- Blankets

Listen for hurricane warnings on the radio or TV, and follow the instructions. The National Hurricane Center

Vehicles leave New Orleans ahead of Hurricane Katrina on August 28, 2005. Road signs (inset) often inform people of evacuation routes.

also posts hurricane warnings on its Web site (see Further Reading section). If the local officials say you should evacuate, leave as quickly as you can.

If a Hurricane Is Coming

If a hurricane warning is issued for your area, damage to you and your home can be reduced if your family does the following:

- Nail boards over your home's windows.
- Pick up toys, bikes, and other objects outside the house. Put them where they will not blow around and cause damage.
- Prevent flooding by placing sandbags around your house.
- Trim bushes and tree limbs hanging over the house.
- Inside the house, put strips of duct tape crisscross on windows to keep broken glass from flying around.
- Fill bathtubs, pails, and bottles with water for drinking and washing. The water supply may be cut off or polluted.

Unless there is an evacuation, stay inside your home. Do not leave even if it seems like the storm is over. Remember, it could be the eye of the storm. A hurricane is not over until the second half of the storm has passed.

Hurricanes are terrifying disasters, but learning about them can help you be prepared. Knowing where to go and what to do if a hurricane strikes can make a huge difference in keeping you and your family safe.

CHAPTER NOTES

CHAPTER 1   KATRINA HITS NEW
ORLEANS

1. "Climate of 2005: Summary of Hurricane Katrina," *National Climatic Data Center (NCDC)*, December 29, 2005, <http://www.ncdc.noaa.gov/oa/climate/research/2005/katrina.html> (June 27, 2007).

2. Ibid.

3. David L. Johnson, "Service Assessment: Hurricane Katrina August 23-31, 2005," *NOAA's National Weather Service*, June 2006, <http://www.weather.gov/om/assessments/pdfs/Katrina.pdf> (August 19, 2008).

4. "Climate of 2005: Summary of Hurricane Katrina."

5. Axel Graumann, Tamara Houston, et al., "Hurricane Katrina: A Climatological Perspective," *Technical Report 2005-01, NOAA's National Climatic Data Center*, August 2006, <http://www.ncdc.noaa.gov/oa/reports/tech-report-200501z.pdf> (August 19, 2008).

6. Ibid.

7. Ibid.

8. Ibid.

CHAPTER 3   UNDERSTANDING
HURRICANES

1. Gretchen Cook-Anderson and Krishna Ramanujan, "Researchers Seeing Double on African Monsoons," *Goddard Space Flight Center, NASA*, June 10, 2004, <http://www.nasa.gov/centers/goddard/news/topstory/2004/0510africanwaves.html> (April 11, 2008).

2. Craig Pittman, "Storm's Howl Fills the Ears of Survivors," *St. Petersburg Times*, August 18, 2002, <http://www.sptimes.com/2002/webspecials02/andrew/day1/story1.shtml> (April 16, 2008).

CHAPTER 4   WHEN A HURRICANE HITS

1. "Hurricanes, Typhoons, Cyclones: Backgrounder," The National Center for Atmospheric Research & the UCAR Office of Programs, June 2007, <http://www.ucar.edu/news/backgrounders/hurricanes.jsp> (July 19, 2007).

2. "NOAA's Hurricane Story Ideas," *National Oceanic & Atmospheric Administration (NOAA)*, March 27, 2001, <http://hurricanes.noaa.gov/stories.html> (July 26, 2007).

3. "Hurricanes: Unleashing Nature's Fury," *National Oceanic & Atmospheric Administration (NOAA)*, August 2001, <http://www.nws.noaa.gov/om/brochures/hurr.pdf> (July 26, 2007).

4. "After 10 Years, Hurricane Andrew Gains Strength," *NOAA Magazine*, August 21, 2002, <http://www.noaanews.noaa.gov/stories/s966.htm> (April 16, 2008).

5. Tom Ross, "National Oceanic and Atmospheric Association: Climate-Watch, August, 1999," *NOAA/National Climatic Data Center*, September 15, 1999, <http://www.ncdc.noaa.gov/oa/climate/extremes/1999/august/extremes0899.html> (April 16, 2008).

6. Ed Rappaport, "Preliminary Report: Hurricane Andrew 16–28 August 1992," *National Oceanic & Atmospheric Administration* (NOAA), December 25, 1998, <http://www.nhc.noaa.gov/1992andrew.html> (July 26, 2007).

7. Frank Jack Daniel, "Up to 1000 May Be Buried Under Mudslides," *The New Zealand Herald*, October 9, 2005, <http://www.nws.noaa.gov/om/assessments/pdfs/Katrina.pdf> (April 16, 2008).

8. David L. Johnson, "Hurricane Katrina August 23–31, 2005," *NOAA's National Weather Service*, June 2006, <http://www.nws.noaa.gov/om/assessments/pdfs/Katrina.pdf> (July 27, 2007).

9. P. J. Webster, G. J. Holland, J. A. Curry, and H.R. Chang, "Changes in Tropical Cyclone Number, Duration, and Intensity in a Warming Environment," *Science*, September 16, 2005, p. 1846.

CHAPTER 5 TRACKING HURRICANES

1. Ron Trumbla, "The Great Galveston Hurricane of 1900," *NOAA Celebrates 200 Years of Science, Service, and Stewardship*, August 31, 2007, <http://celebrating200years.noaa.gov/magazine/galv_hurricane/> (September 17, 2008).

2. Neal Dorst, "Hurricane Timeline," *National Oceanic and Atmospheric Administration FAQ: Hurricanes, Typhoons, and Tropical Cyclones*, June 1, 2007, <http://www.aoml.noaa.gov/hrd/tcfaq/J6.html> (July 31, 2007).

3. NOAA, "Predicting Hurricanes: Times Have Changed," *NOAA Celebrates 200 Years of Science, Service, and Stewardship*, August 1, 2007, <http://celebrating200years.noaa.gov/magazine/devast_hurricane/welcome.html> (April 15, 2008).

4. Associated Press, "Flash Flooding Swamps Many Houston Area Streets," *KHOU.com: News for Houston Texas*, September 14, 2008, <http://www.khou.com/topstories/stories/khou080912_tj_houston_ike_hurricane.659ae065.html> (September 17, 2008).

CHAPTER 6 STAYING SAFE

1. "Facts for Features: *Special Edition* 2007 Hurricane Season Begins," *U.S. Census Bureau*, May 22, 2007, <http://www.census.gov/PressRelease/www/releases/archives/facts_for_features_special_editions/010106.html> (July 31, 2007).

GLOSSARY

air masses—Portions of the atmosphere that move around the Earth.

air pressure—The force exerted by the molecules of the atmosphere.

condense—Change from a gas into a liquid.

Coriolis effect—An apparent shift of winds to the west, due to the Earth's rotation.

easterly wave—A westward-moving disturbance in the winds blowing near the equator.

evacuate—Move to safety.

evaporate—Change from a liquid to a gas as the temperature is raised.

eye—A low-pressure area of calm air at the center of a hurricane.

eyewall—The edge of the eye of a hurricane; contains the strongest winds and heaviest rains.

high-pressure system—A weather system in which winds from high altitudes blow down at the Earth's surface to bring calm weather.

landfall—Arrival at land.

levee—A wall built from sand and dirt, designed to prevent flooding.

low-pressure system—A weather system in which rising, swirling warm air currents form clouds and bring unstable, stormy weather.

meteorologist—A scientist who studies weather.

precipitation—Water vapor in a liquid or solid state that falls to the Earth's surface in the form of rain, snow, sleet, or hail.

rainbands—Bands of thick clouds swirling out from the eye of a hurricane; produce heavy rainfalls.

sublimation—The changing of a solid to a gas.

storm surge—A sudden rise in the water of oceans, lakes, or rivers that is pushed to shore by the strong winds swirling around a storm.

tornado—A violent storm in the form of a funnel of spinning air.

tropical cyclone—A large storm with circular wind movement and low pressure at the center, over a tropical ocean.

water vapor—Water as a gas.

FURTHER READING

BOOKS

Fraden, Dennis and Judith, *Witness to Disaster: Hurricanes*. Des Moines, IA: National Geographic Children's Books, 2007.

Park, Louise, *Hurricanes*. North Mankato, MN: Smart Apple Media, 2008.

Treaster, Joseph B., *Hurricane Force: In the Path of the America's Deadliest Storms*. Boston, MA: Kingfisher, 2007.

Woods, Michael, and Mary Woods. *Hurricanes*. Minneapolis, Minn.: Lerner Publications Company, 2007.

INTERNET ADDRESSES

Hurricane Photos, National Geographic
<http://kids.nationalgeographic.com/Photos/Gallery/Hurricanes>
Includes vivid color photos of hurricanes.

"Hurricanes," FEMA for Kids
<http://www.fema.gov/kids/hurr.htm>
Includes hurricane facts, stories, cartoons, and canine heroes trading cards.

National Hurricane Center
<http://www.nhc.noaa.gov/>

"Tropical Twisters—Hurricanes: How They Work and What They Do," NASA
<http://kids.earth.nasa.gov/archive/hurricane/>
Has a virtual reality tour of a hurricane, and a link to the Hurricane Hunters site.

INDEX